Revolting Arithmetic: Tudors

Rowland Morgan

Revolting Arithmetic: Tudors

A Tudor monk selling pardons

Editor: Sarah Hall
Illustrations: Andrew Noble – Andrew Noble Design Team Ltd
                     Gary Clifford – The Drawing Room (illustrations on pages 14, 15 and 16)
Layout artist: Jane Conway
Cover image: Andrew Noble
Cover design: Ed Gallagher

© 2000 Belair Publications, on behalf of the author.

Every effort has been made to contact copyright holders of material used in this book. If any have been overlooked, we will be pleased to make any necessary arrangements.

First published 2000 by Belair Publications, Dunstable.

Belair Publications, Albert House, Apex Business Centre, Boscombe Road, Dunstable, LU5 4RL, England.

ISBN 1–84191–037–6

Printed in Singapore by Craft Print Pte Ltd.

Contents

Lovely Grub

Roast peacock for dinner in Tudor times

Introduction

Cross-curricular maths

Most people agree that there is a maths problem in Britain. Pupils tend not to like it much, teachers are in short supply and results could be better. Maths is not as popular as it could be. Sadly, that has been taken for granted.

Why has maths got a bad name when, of all the subjects in primary school, maths is the one where there is often a definite right answer or a wrong one? It is the subject in which you can learn an operation, perform it and get marks. It is quite straightforward.

People use maths all the time. In a game of darts, working out a knitting pattern, checking bank accounts – there are so many ways people enjoy their command of numbers, without thinking about it.

Revolting Arithmetic takes a shot at motivating children's enjoyment of maths by integrating parts of it with history. Historians may frown. Mathematicians may raise an eyebrow. Children will just say: cross-curricular, here we come!

How to use this book

These activities are intended to help children practise their mathematics in the context of work on historical topics. They could be used for homework or for additional mathematical work outside the daily maths lesson. You may want children to write directly on the sheets, or they may be used as resource material, with pupils recording their answers elsewhere.

To give the flexibility to match the activities to work in different year groups or to children of differing ability, the copiable activity pages are laid out in three gradations of difficulty.

Level 1 uses mathematical operations (mostly arithmetic) at a level roughly equivalent to Year 3. This should suit most children in Years 3–4. Level 2 is more appropriate to Years 4–5. Level 3 is aimed at Years 5–6.

There is a self-checking function on each sheet in which we sometimes push the agenda a little, in the hope that self-marking will motivate some stretching. You may want some children to use a calculator for this. Answers and algorithms are provided at the back of the book.

The Tudors

Under the Tudors, the kingdom of England moved from the medieval era into the Renaissance. Change brought widespread poverty and suffering. The court showed brutal indifference to those maimed in its many wars. In their turn, typhus and the plague were indifferent to wealth and status. In order to build the expanding navy, vast areas of forest were felled for iron and timber. Out of this

dangerous, greedy and fanatical age arose some of the most dramatic chapters of history: religious revolution, invasion and empire. It was also the age of new technology in the form of the printing press. During the Tudor Age, England and Wales became a world power. The remarkable Tudor dynasty has an enduring appeal for children.

Bosworth Field

The Tudor Age began in 1485 with a shock victory in battle. It was the last time an English king died at war. King Richard the Third had made many enemies. One of these was Henry Tudor. They fought a battle at Bosworth Field. Richard was killed. Henry took the crown from his body and became King Henry the Seventh, the first Tudor king.

JUST MY SIZE

1 Henry Tudor landed in Wales with two thousand French soldiers. Write that number in figures.

2 If Wales added 750 soldiers to Henry's army and Cornwall added 95, how many extra was that altogether?

3 King Richard had 10 000 men and Henry Tudor had 5000. How many times more men did King Richard have?

TUDOR FACT FILE
During the battle, the King attacked and nearly killed Henry. But he was betrayed by enemies in his own army who helped Henry win.

WALES ENGLAND

4 If half of King Richard's troops did not fight, what fraction did?

CHECK IT YOURSELF ✔

Your answer to 1 → ☐ ☐ ☐ ☐

Your answer to 2 ——→ **8** ☐ ☐

Your answer to 3 ———————→ ☐

Add them Result → **2** **8** ☐ ☐

Do you get **2847**? *If not, check your answers and try again.*

Bosworth Field

The Tudor Age began in 1485 with a shock victory in battle. It was the last time an English king died at war. King Richard the Third had taken the throne from twelve-year-old King Edward. This had made him many enemies. One of these was Henry Tudor. They fought a battle at Bosworth Field. Richard was killed. Henry took the crown from his body and became King Henry the Seventh, the first Tudor king.

1 Henry Tudor landed in Wales with two thousand and twenty-eight French soldiers. The King had twelve thousand and ninety. Write out the bigger number in figures.

2 Henry gathered soldiers on his way into England. If Wales added 758 and Cornwall added 396, how many extra soldiers was that?

3 If King Richard had 900 cavalry and Henry Tudor had 250, how many more cavalry did King Richard have?

TUDOR FACT FILE
During the battle, enemies betrayed King Richard. The King attacked and nearly killed Henry, but Earl Stanley joined Henry's side and the Earl of Northumberland held back his troops. This helped Henry win.

4 If half of King Richard's troops held back, what decimal fraction was left to fight?

CHECK IT YOURSELF ✔

Your answer to 1 ⟶ ☐☐☐☐☐

Your answer to 2 ⟶ 1 ☐☐☐

Your answer to 3 ⟶ ☐☐☐

Add them/Result ⟶ 1 3 ☐☐☐

Do you get **13 894**? *If not, check your answers and try again.*

Revolting Arithmetic: Tudors

Bosworth Field

The Tudor Age began in 1485 with a shock victory in battle. It was the last time an English king died at war, or that his successor took the crown from his fallen body. King Richard the Third had seized the throne from twelve-year-old King Edward. This had made him many enemies. Henry Tudor, from a rival family, saw his chance. He fought with Richard at the Battle of Bosworth Field. Richard was killed. Henry took the crown from his body and became King Henry the Seventh, the first Tudor king.

JUST MY SIZE

1 Henry Tudor sailed from Brittany and landed in Wales with two thousand and twenty-eight French soldiers. If the King had twelve thousand and ninety, how many more troops did the King have?

2 Henry gathered forces on his way into England. If Wales added 1400 and England added 1650, how many extra soldiers was that?

3 The armies fought for two hours. If King Richard lost 20 per cent of his 1000 cavalry, how many were left?

TUDOR FACT FILE
During the battle, enemies betrayed King Richard. His main general, the Duke of Norfolk, was soon killed. The King attacked and nearly killed Henry, but Earl Stanley joined Henry's side and the Earl of Northumberland held back his troops. This helped Henry win.

WALES ENGLAND

4 If 50 per cent of King Richard's 12 000 troops held back, how many were left to fight?

CHECK IT YOURSELF ✓

Your answer to 1 ⟶ ☐☐☐☐☐

Your answer to 2 ⟶ ☐☐☐☐

Your answer to 3 ⟶ ☐☐☐

Your answer to 4 ⟶ ☐☐☐

Add them   Result ⟶ ☐☐☐☐

Do you get **19 912**? *If not, check your answers and try again.*

Lavish Living

The future King Henry the Eighth had food delivered to his rooms twice a day. The food was for Henry and his servants. Look at the list below to see what each delivery consisted of.

PLEASE SUPPLY

Loaves	12
Dishes of meat	6
Gallons of ale	8
Barrels of wine	1

twice daily

IT'S ALRIGHT FOR SOME

1 How many loaves did he receive per day?

2 How many gallons of ale did he receive per day?

3 If Henry and his ten servants each had two mugs of ale per day, how many did they have altogether?

4 How many barrels of wine did they receive per week?

TUDOR FACT FILE
Tudor nobles drank 300 barrels of wine and 600 000 gallons of beer and ale a year. Tudor cooks roasted a peacock then put its feathers back on. It was served complete with a golden beak, which the King ate.

CHECK IT YOURSELF ✔

Your answer to 1 ———➤ ☐ ☐

Your answer to 2 ———➤ ☐ ☐

Your answer to 3 ———➤ ☐ ☐

Your answer to 4 ———➤ ☐ ☐

Add them   Result ———➤ ☐ ☐

*Do you get **76**? If not, check your answers and try again.*

Revolting Arithmetic: *Tudors*

Lavish Living

As Prince of Wales, the future King Henry the Eighth had food delivered to his rooms **twice** a day. The food was for Henry and his ten servants. Look at the list below to see what each delivery consisted of.

IT'S ALRIGHT FOR SOME

PLEASE SUPPLY

Loaves	12
Dishes of meat	6
Gallons of ale	8
Barrels of wine	1

1 How many loaves did he receive per week?

2 How many gallons of ale did he receive per week?

3 If Henry and his ten servants each had two mugs of ale per day, how many did they have altogether per week?

4 If each dish of meat held 12 pieces, how many pieces **each** were there in one delivery for Henry and his servants, in round numbers?

5 If the barrels of wine contained 15 litres, how many litres came each week?

TUDOR FACT FILE

Tudor nobles drank 300 barrels of wine and 600 000 gallons of beer and ale a year. Tudor cooks roasted a peacock then put its feathers back on. It was served complete with a golden beak, which the King ate.

CHECK IT YOURSELF ✔

Your answer to 1 ⟶ ☐ ☐ ☐

Your answer to 2 ⟶ ☐ ☐ ☐

Your answer to 3 ⟶ ☐ ☐ ☐

Your answer to 4 ⟶ ☐

Your answer to 5 ⟶ ☐ ☐ ☐

Add them   Result ⟶ ☐ ☐ ☐

*Do you get **651**? If not, check your answers and try again.*

Lavish Living

As Prince of Wales, the future King Henry the Eighth had food delivered to his rooms at the royal palace **twice** a day. The food was for Henry and his ten servants. Look at the list below to see what each delivery consisted of.

PLEASE SUPPLY

Loaves	12
Dishes of meat	6
Gallons of ale	8
Barrels of wine	1

IT'S ALRIGHT FOR SOME

1 How many loaves did he receive per person per week (in round numbers)?

2 How many gallons of ale did he receive per person per week (in round numbers)?

3 If Henry and his servants drank seven and a half gallons of ale per day, how much was left over for the kitchen staff each week?

4 If each dish of meat held 50 pieces, how many pieces **each** were there per delivery for Henry and his servants (in round numbers)?

5 If the barrels of wine contained 15 litres, how many litres came each fortnight?

TUDOR FACT FILE
Tudor nobles drank 300 barrels of wine and 600 000 gallons of beer and ale a year. Tudor cooks roasted a peacock then put its feathers back on. It was served to the lords and ladies complete with a golden beak, which the monarch ate.

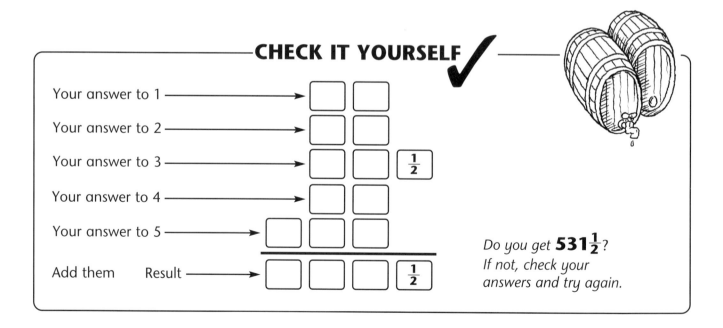

CHECK IT YOURSELF ✔

Your answer to 1 ⟶ ☐ ☐

Your answer to 2 ⟶ ☐ ☐

Your answer to 3 ⟶ ☐ ☐ $\frac{1}{2}$

Your answer to 4 ⟶ ☐ ☐

Your answer to 5 ⟶ ☐ ☐ ☐

Add them   Result ⟶ ☐ ☐ ☐ $\frac{1}{2}$

Do you get **531$\frac{1}{2}$**?
If not, check your answers and try again.

Monks and Money

In Tudor times, people believed that they could buy forgiveness for their sins. The greedy monks took people's money and in return handed out papers which people thought were tickets to heaven.

1 Monks had a special sale in the year fifteen hundred and seventeen. Write out the year in figures.

2 Everybody wanted to buy a ticket. Imagine one ticket cost 40 shillings. How many shillings would it cost to buy tickets for a family of three?

STATELLITE	
Monasteries built	
before 1000:	94
1000–1099:	37
1100–1199:	500
1200–1299:	556
1300–1399:	12
1400–1499:	13

3 Rich people who became monks gave all they had to the monastery. If one man gave 765 acres and another gave 98 acres, how many acres of land would the monastery gain?

4 Look at the chart. In which century were the most monasteries built? (Remember: the 15th century is the 1400s.)

CHECK IT YOURSELF ✔

Your answer to 1 → ☐ ☐ ☐ ☐

Your answer to 2 → **1** ☐ ☐

Your answer to 3 → **8** ☐ ☐

Your answer to 4 (number only) → ☐ ☐

Add them   Result → **2** **5** ☐ ☐

Do you get **2513**? *If not, check your answers and try again.*

Monks and Money

In Tudor times, people believed that they could buy forgiveness for their sins. The greedy monks took people's money and in return handed out papers which they said pardoned their sins. People thought these papers were tickets to heaven.

1 Monks had a special sale of pardons in 1517 to help rebuild the Church of Saint Peter in Rome. If monks kept back 0.5 of a sale worth 45 shillings, how much would go to Rome?

2 Everybody wanted to buy a pardon. Imagine one pardon cost 45 shillings. How many shillings would it cost to buy tickets to heaven for a family of four grandparents, two parents and three children?

STATELLITE
Monasteries built

before 1000:	94
1000–1099:	37
1100–1199:	500
1200–1299:	556
1300–1399:	12
1400–1499:	13

3 When rich people became monks, they gave their wealth to the monastery. So, although monks had no money, monasteries were rich. If a rich man gave 765 acres and another gave 398 acres, how many acres of land would the monastery gain?

4 Look at the chart of monastery building. How many monasteries were built in the 12th and 13th centuries? (Remember: the 12th century is the 1100s.)

CHECK IT YOURSELF ✔

Your answer to 1 ⟶ ☐ ☐ . **5**

Your answer to 2 ⟶ ☐ ☐ ☐

Your answer to 3 ⟶ ☐ ☐ ☐ ☐

Your answer to 4 ⟶ ☐ ☐ ☐ ☐

Add them Result ⟶ **2** ☐ ☐ ☐ . **5**

*Do you get **2646.5**? If not, check your answers and try again.*

Monks and Money

In Tudor times, people believed that they could buy forgiveness for their sins. The greedy monks took people's money and in return handed out papers which they said pardoned their sins. People believed the monks and thought that these papers were tickets to heaven.

1 Monks had a special sale of pardons in the year 1517 to help rebuild the Church of Saint Peter in Rome. If monks kept back 50 per cent of a sale worth 37 shillings, how much would they earn?

2 Everybody wanted to buy a ticket to heaven and the monasteries made a lot of money. Imagine one of the monks' documents cost 37 shillings. How many shillings would it cost to buy tickets to heaven for a family of four grandparents, two parents and seven children?

STATELLITE	
Monasteries built	
before 1000:	94
1000–1099:	37
1100–1199:	500
1200–1299:	556
1300–1399:	12
1400–1499:	13

3 When rich people became monks, they gave all their wealth to the monastery. So, although monks had no money, monasteries were rich. If a rich man gave 1765 acres and another gave 1398 acres, how many acres of land would the monastery gain?

4 Look at the chart of monastery building. How many more monasteries were built in the 12th than in the 11th century?

CHECK IT YOURSELF ✓

Your answer to 1 ⟶ ☐ ☐ . ☐ ☐

Your answer to 2 ⟶ ☐ ☐ ☐

Your answer to 3 ⟶ ☐ ☐ ☐ ☐

Your answer to 4 ⟶ ☐ ☐ ☐

Add them/Result ⟶ ☐ ☐ ☐ ☐ . ☐ ☐

*Do you get **4125.50**? If not, check your answers and try again.*

Greedy Henry

In the 1530s, King Henry the Eighth took all the church lands and sold the monasteries. It changed the country for ever.

1 Church monasteries owned one-quarter of the land. What fraction of the land was left for others?

2 There were a thousand and twelve monasteries. Write out that number in figures.

Abbey

Abbey farmhouse

Abbot's palace

TUDOR FACT FILE
Henry the Eighth showed off his wealth from the monasteries. Hampton Court Palace was crammed with treasures. Every day the banqueting hall was filled with fresh tapestries and new stacks of silver plate.

3 Look at the plan of a monastic estate. If the King's men burn down the abbey in ten estates like this, how many buildings are left to sell?

4 If the King sells the abbot's palace for £95 and the rest of the estate sells for £985, how much does the King get?

CHECK IT YOURSELF ✓

Your answer to 2 → ☐ ☐ ☐ ☐

Your answer to 3 —————→ ☐ ☐

Your answer to 4 → **1** **0** ☐ ☐

Add them   Result → **2** **1** ☐ ☐

Do you get **2112**? *If not, check your answers and try again.*

Greedy Henry

In the 1530s, King Henry the Eighth took all the church lands and sold the monasteries to his friends. It changed the country for ever.

1 If church monasteries owned 0.3 of the land, what decimal fraction of the land was left for others?

2 If there were 807 small monasteries and 205 large ones, how many were there altogether?

3 Look at the plan of a monastic estate. If the King's men take all the area of land shown, how many acres does the King get?

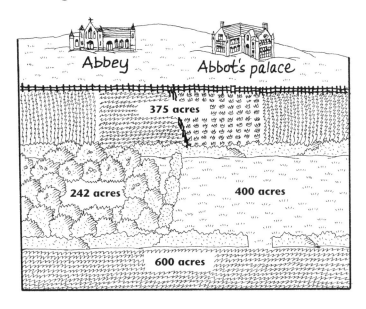

TUDOR FACT FILE
Henry the Eighth expanded Hampton Court Palace to show off his wealth from the monasteries. He had it crammed with treasures. Every day the banqueting hall was hung with fresh tapestries and piled high with new stacks of silver plate.

4 If the abbot's palace sells to one of the King's friends for £986 and the rest of the estate sells for £765, how much does the King get?

CHECK IT YOURSELF ✔

Your answer to 2 ⟶ **1** ☐ ☐ ☐

Your answer to 3 ⟶ **1** ☐ ☐ ☐

Your answer to 4 ⟶ **1** ☐ ☐ ☐

Add them/Result ⟶ **4** ☐ ☐ ☐

Do you get **4380**?
If not, check your answers and try again.

Greedy Henry

In the 1530s, King Henry the Eighth seized all the church lands and sold the monasteries to his friends. It changed the country for ever.

1 Church monasteries owned 25 per cent of the land. What percentage of the land was left for others?

2 There were a thousand and twelve monasteries. If 807 of them were small monasteries, how many large ones were there?

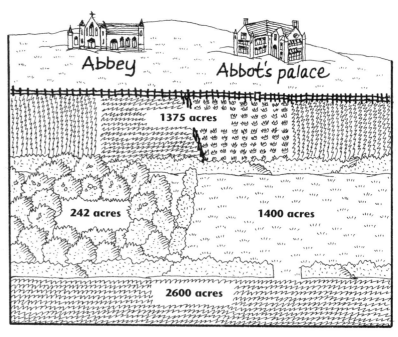

Abbey   Abbot's palace

1375 acres

242 acres   1400 acres

2600 acres

TUDOR FACT FILE

Hampton Court Palace was expanded by Henry the Eighth to show off his wealth after he plundered the monasteries. He had it crammed with treasures. Every day the banqueting hall was hung with fresh tapestries and piled high with new stacks of silver plate to humble his visitors.

3 Look at the plan of a monastic estate. If the King's men take all the area of land shown, how many acres does the King get?

4 If the abbot's palace sells to one of the King's friends for £1387 and the rest of the estate sells for £1899, how much goes into the King's treasury?

CHECK IT YOURSELF ✓

Your answer to 1 ⟶ ☐ ☐

Your answer to 2 ⟶ ☐ ☐ ☐

Your answer to 3 ⟶ ☐ ☐ ☐ ☐

Your answer to 4 ⟶ ☐ ☐ ☐ ☐

Add them   Result ⟶ ☐ ☐ ☐ ☐

*Do you get **9183**? If not, check your answers and try again.*

Pilgrimage of Grace

When King Henry took the monasteries, many people were made homeless and began to starve. A big crowd gathered in York. They called their protest the Pilgrimage of Grace. King Henry put the leaders to death to frighten the others.

Homeless people	
Abbey 1	74
Abbey 2	83
Abbey 3	59
Duke's estate	34

1 If the homeless sent away from Abbey 1 and Abbey 2 were among the crowd, how many people was that?

2 How many homeless people came from the abbeys and the duke's estate altogether?

3 Suppose there were nine hundred and seventy-six people in the crowd. Write that number in figures.

4 If 35 people from the three abbeys and the duke's estate were hanged, how many were left?

CHECK IT YOURSELF ✔

Your answer to 1 ⟶ | **1** | | |

Your answer to 2 ⟶ | **2** | | |

Your answer to 3 ⟶ | **9** | | |

Your answer to 4 ⟶ | **2** | | |

Add them   Result ⟶ | **1** | **5** | | |

Do you get **1598**? *If not, check your answers and try again.*

Pilgrimage of Grace

When King Henry closed the monasteries, many people were made homeless. People began to starve. In 1536 many homeless people gathered in York to demand justice from the King. They called their protest the Pilgrimage of Grace. King Henry promised the people a pardon and a parliament at York if they went away, but later he had the leaders put to death to frighten the others.

Homeless people	
Abbey 1	108
Abbey 2	129
Abbey 3	96
Duke's estate	42

1 If the homeless sent away from Abbey 1 and Abbey 2 were among the crowd which gathered in York, how many people was that?

2 How many homeless people came from the abbeys and the duke's estate altogether?

3 Forty thousand people occupied York. Write that number in figures.

4 If a quarter of the people from Abbey 3 were hanged, how many were left from that abbey?

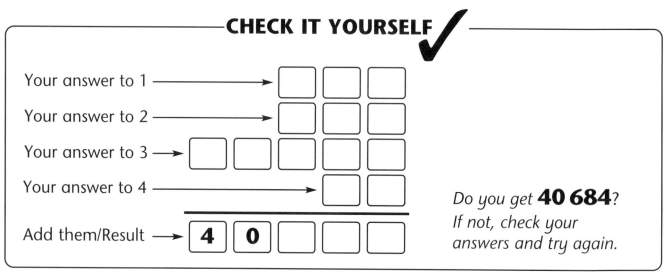

CHECK IT YOURSELF ✔

Your answer to 1 ⟶ ☐ ☐ ☐

Your answer to 2 ⟶ ☐ ☐ ☐

Your answer to 3 ⟶ ☐ ☐ ☐ ☐ ☐

Your answer to 4 ⟶ ☐ ☐

Add them/Result ⟶ **4** **0** ☐ ☐ ☐

Do you get **40 684**? *If not, check your answers and try again.*

Revolting Arithmetic: *Tudors* © Belair (copiable page)

Pilgrimage of Grace

When King Henry the Eighth closed the monasteries, many people were made homeless and sheep were put onto their land instead. People began to starve. In 1536 many homeless people gathered in York to demand justice from the King. They called their protest the Pilgrimage of Grace. At first, King Henry promised the people a pardon and a parliament at York if they went away. However, as more crowds gathered, King Henry had the leaders put to death to frighten the others.

Homeless people	
Abbey 1	1108
Abbey 2	1129
Abbey 3	796
Duke's estate	242

1 If the homeless sent away from Abbey 1 and Abbey 2 were among the crowd which gathered in York, how many people was that?

2 How many homeless people came from the abbeys and the duke's estate altogether?

3 In 1536, forty thousand people occupied York. How many people came besides the ones from the abbeys and the duke's estate?

4 If a quarter of the people from Abbey 3 were hanged, how many were left from that abbey?

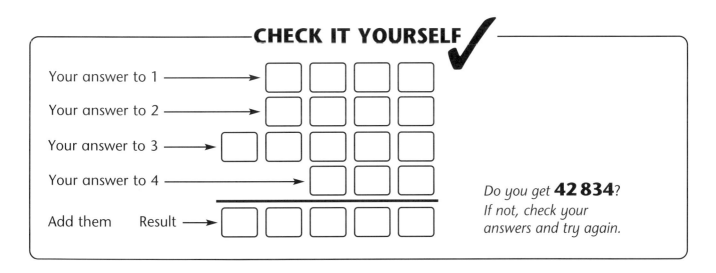

CHECK IT YOURSELF ✔

Your answer to 1 ⟶ ☐☐☐☐

Your answer to 2 ⟶ ☐☐☐☐

Your answer to 3 ⟶ ☐☐☐☐☐

Your answer to 4 ⟶ ☐☐☐

Add them   Result ⟶ ☐☐☐☐☐

Do you get **42 834**? *If not, check your answers and try again.*

Thomas Cromwell

Thomas Cromwell was a politician. He arranged for Henry the Eighth to marry Anne of Cleves but Henry hated her. Cromwell was beheaded in the Tower of London.

1 Cromwell shut down nine hundred and twenty monasteries in just four years. Write that number in figures.

2 Sir Richard Rich got rich by helping Cromwell – and himself. He grabbed 59 manors, 31 rectories and 28 vicarages. How many properties is that?

3 The Holy Bible was translated into English in 1535. Four years later, Cromwell ordered that a Bible should be supplied to each parish. In what year was that?

4 Henry married Anne of Cleves in January 1540. The marriage ended in June. During how many months were they married?

WHOOPS!

TUDOR FACT FILE
The Holy Bible had always been in Latin. In the new church, the Bible was in English. A priest named Miles Coverdale translated it.

CHECK IT YOURSELF ✔

Your answer to 1 ⟶ ☐ ☐ ☐

Your answer to 2 ⟶ **1** ☐ ☐

Your answer to 3 ⟶ **1** **5** ☐ ☐

Your answer to 4 ⟶ ☐

Add them   Result ⟶ **2** **5** ☐ ☐

Do you get **2583**?
If not, check your answers and try again.

Revolting Arithmetic: *Tudors*   © Belair (copiable page)

Thomas Cromwell

THOMAS CROMWELL

Thomas Cromwell was a Tudor politician. He set up the new Church of England and ran it for the King. He arranged for Henry the Eighth to marry Anne of Cleves but Henry hated her. Cromwell was sent to the Tower of London to be beheaded.

1 Cromwell and his officials shut down nine hundred and twenty monasteries in the first four years. If they shut 119 the next year, how many was that altogether?

2 Sir Richard Rich got rich by helping Cromwell – and himself. He grabbed 59 manors, 31 rectories and 28 vicarages. If he divided the vicarages equally among his four children, how many did each of them inherit?

3 The Holy Bible had been translated into English in 1535. In 1539, Cromwell ordered that a Bible should be supplied to each parish. By that time, for how many years had the Bible been available in English?

4 If 258 Bibles were delivered in one week to churches in Wales and 983 in England, how many is that altogether?

WHOOPS!

> **TUDOR FACT FILE**
> The Holy Bible had always been in Latin. In the new church, the Bible was in English. A priest named Miles Coverdale translated it.

✔ CHECK IT YOURSELF

Your answer to 1 ——→ **1** ☐ ☐ ☐

Your answer to 2 —————————→ ☐

Your answer to 3 —————————→ ☐

Your answer to 4 ——→ **1** ☐ ☐ ☐

Add them   Result ——→ **2** ☐ ☐ ☐

Do you get **2291**? *If not, check your answers and try again.*

Revolting Arithmetic: *Tudors*

Thomas Cromwell

Thomas Cromwell was a Tudor politician. The common folk hated him for shutting down the monasteries in order to make the King rich. He set up the new Church of England and ran it for the King. He arranged for Henry the Eighth to marry Anne of Cleves but the King hated her. Cromwell was sent to the Tower of London to be beheaded.

1 Thomas Cromwell and his officials shut down nine hundred and twenty monasteries in the first four years. How many was that per year on average?

2 Sir Richard Rich was one of the many landlords who got rich helping Cromwell – and himself. He grabbed 59 manors, 31 rectories and 28 vicarages. If he divided the properties equally among his four children, how many properties were left over?

3 In 1539, Cromwell decreed that a Holy Bible should be supplied to each parish. If, say, 1098 Bibles were delivered to churches in Wales in one year and 3499 in England, how many is that altogether?

4 If Cromwell could have 25 Bibles printed every day, how many days would it take to supply 8000?

TUDOR FACT FILE
The Holy Bible had always been in Latin. In the new royal church, the Bible was in English. A priest named Miles Coverdale translated it in 1535.

CHECK IT YOURSELF ✔

Your answer to 1 ⟶ ☐ ☐ ☐

Your answer to 2 ⟶ ☐

Your answer to 3 ⟶ ☐ ☐ ☐ ☐

Your answer to 4 ⟶ ☐ ☐ ☐

Add them   Result ⟶ ☐ ☐ ☐ ☐

*Do you get **5149**? If not, check your answers and try again.*

Revolting Arithmetic: *Tudors*

Tudor Punishments

Imagine these are the punishments given out by a Tudor justice of the peace in one day.

Arthur Brown	Stole a sheep	2 days pillory
May Jones	Witchcraft	3 days pillory
Christopher Birch	Stole food	1 day pillory
Rosa Lee	Stole a gown	2 days pillory
James Drew	Bullied his neighbours	30 lashes
Richard Green	Assaulted constable	50 lashes
Antony Wade	Drunk	Five shillings fine
William Hyde	Drunk and loud	Seven shillings fine
Timothy White	Trading without licence	14 shillings fine
John Drummond	Illegal printing	25 shillings fine
Stephen Teacher	Stole apple	Two days in irons
Harold Smith	Stole bun	One day in irons

1 How many days in the pillory did he give out?

2 How many lashes did he order?

3 How many shillings in fines did he impose?

4 How many **hours** in irons did he order?

CHECK IT YOURSELF ✓

Your answer to 1 ⟶ ▢

Your answer to 2 ⟶ ▢ ▢

Your answer to 3 ⟶ ▢ ▢

Your answer to 4 ⟶ ▢ ▢

Add them Result ⟶ ▢ ▢ ▢

Do you get **211**?
If not, check your answers and try again.

Tudor Punishments

Imagine these are the sentences imposed by a Tudor justice of the peace (magistrate) in a working day.

Arthur Brown	Stole a sheep	2 days pillory
May Jones	Witchcraft	3 days pillory
Christopher Birch	Stole food	1 day pillory
Rosa Lee	Stole a gown	2 days pillory
James Drew	Bullied his neighbours	130 lashes
Richard Green	Assaulted constable	150 lashes
Antony Wade	Drunk	Five shillings fine
William Hyde	Drunk and loud	Seven shillings fine
Timothy White	Trading without licence	14 shillings fine
John Drummond	Illegal printing	25 shillings fine
Stephen Teacher	Stole apple	Two days in irons
Harold Smith	Stole bun	One day in irons

1 How many **hours** in the pillory did he give out?

2 How many lashes did he order?

3 If this was a typical day,
   a) How many shillings in fines did he impose per five-day working week?
   b) How many **hours** in irons did he order per working week?
   c) How many cases did he handle per month (four weeks)?

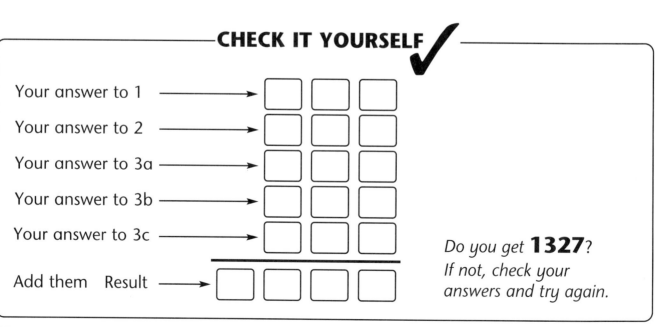

CHECK IT YOURSELF ✓

Your answer to 1 ⟶ ☐ ☐ ☐

Your answer to 2 ⟶ ☐ ☐ ☐

Your answer to 3a ⟶ ☐ ☐ ☐

Your answer to 3b ⟶ ☐ ☐ ☐

Your answer to 3c ⟶ ☐ ☐ ☐

Add them   Result ⟶ ☐ ☐ ☐ ☐

Do you get **1327**? *If not, check your answers and try again.*

Tudor Punishments

Imagine these are the notes a Tudor justice of the peace (magistrate) might have made, recording the sentences imposed in a working day. If this was a typical day, answer the questions about the sentences he might have given over several days and weeks.

Arthur Brown	Stole a sheep	Pillory, 2 days
May Jones	Witchcraft	Pillory, 3 days
Christopher Birch	Stole food	Pillory, 1 day
Rosa Lee	Stole a gown	Pillory, 2 days
James Drew	Bullied his neighbours	130 lashes
Richard Green	Assaulted constable	150 lashes
Antony Wade	Drunk	Fine five shillings
William Hyde	Drunk and loud	Fine seven shillings
Timothy White	Trading without licence	Fine 14 shillings
John Drummond	Illegal printing	Fine 25 shillings
Stephen Teacher	Stole apple	Two days in irons
Harold Smith	Stole bun	One day in irons

TUDOR FACT FILE
The worst punishment was reserved for people with the wrong religious beliefs. They were tortured and burned alive. Among them was Ann Askew who was broken on the torturer's rack and carried to the stake in a chair in 1546.

1 How many **hours** in the pillory did he give out per five-day working week?

2 How many lashes did he order per week?

3 How many shillings in fines did he impose per month (four working weeks)?

4 How many **hours** in irons did he order per month?

5 How many cases did he handle in six months?

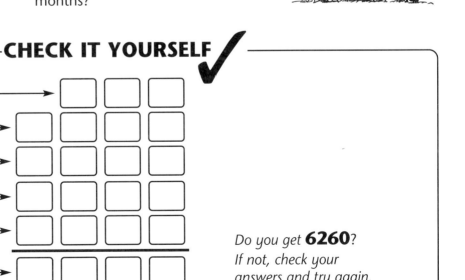

— CHECK IT YOURSELF ✓ —

Your answer to 1 ⟶ ☐ ☐ ☐

Your answer to 2 ⟶ ☐ ☐ ☐

Your answer to 3 ⟶ ☐ ☐ ☐

Your answer to 4 ⟶ ☐ ☐ ☐

Your answer to 5 ⟶ ☐ ☐ ☐

Add them   Result ⟶ ☐ ☐ ☐ ☐

*Do you get **6260**? If not, check your answers and try again.*

Henry the Eighth

King Henry the Eighth was a big man. He hunted all animals. He beat everybody at sports. He built a big navy, got super-rich and bullied the Pope. He was a show-off and very dangerous to work for – or to marry: King Henry the Eighth had six wives.

1 King Henry the Eighth put 158 enemies to death per month. How many is that to the nearest ten?

2 Henry's court at Hampton Court Palace ate about two hundred and five deer a month. Write that number in figures.

TUDOR FACT FILE
One of the world's first tennis courts, built by Henry the Eighth, is still used.

3 Henry was married to his first wife, Catherine of Aragon, for 24 years. This was 10 years more than all the others put together. For how many years altogether was he married to the others?

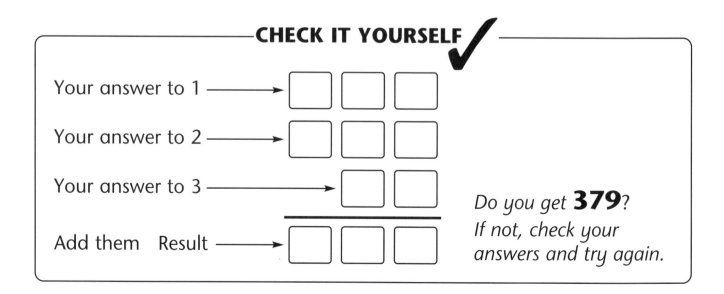

CHECK IT YOURSELF ✔

Your answer to 1 ⟶ ☐☐☐

Your answer to 2 ⟶ ☐☐☐

Your answer to 3 ⟶ ☐☐

Add them   Result ⟶ ☐☐☐

Do you get **379**? *If not, check your answers and try again.*

Henry the Eighth

King Henry the Eighth was a big man. He hunted all animals. He beat everybody at sports. He built a big navy, got super-rich and bullied the Pope. He was a tremendous show-off and very dangerous to work for – or to marry. King Henry had six wives and is notorious for having had two of them beheaded. In many ways, he was larger than life.

1 King Henry the Eighth put his enemies to death at a rate of 5 a day. How many is that in a 30-day month?

2 Henry's merry court at Hampton Court Palace ate about 51 deer a week. How many is that per month?

TUDOR FACT FILE
One of the world's first tennis courts, built by the sporting Henry the Eighth, is still used.

3 Henry was married to his first wife, Catherine of Aragon, for almost 24 years. He married his second wife, Anne Boleyn, in January 1533. Henry died in January 1547, still married to his sixth wife, Catherine Parr. For how many years was he married altogether?

CHECK IT YOURSELF ✔

Your answer to 1 ⟶ ▢▢▢

Your answer to 3 ⟶ ▢▢

Add them   Result ⟶ ▢▢▢

Do you get **188**?
If not, check your answers and try again.

Your answer to 2 ⟶ ▢▢▢

Your answer to 3 ⟶ ▢▢

Add them   Result ⟶ ▢▢▢

Do you get **242**?
If not, check your answers and try again.

Revolting Arithmetic: *Tudors*

Henry the Eighth

King Henry the Eighth was a big man. He hunted all animals. He beat everybody at sports. He built a big navy, got super-rich and bullied the Pope. He was a tremendous show-off and very dangerous to work for – or to marry. King Henry had six wives and is notorious for having had two of them beheaded. In many ways, he was larger than life.

1 King Henry the Eighth put an average of five enemies to death per day. How many enemies did he execute in a year?

2 Nobles at King Henry's merry court in Hampton Court Palace ate 204 deer per month.
   a) If Henry's private table took one-quarter of these, how many is that?
   b) Counting a month as four weeks, how many deer went to the King's table each week (to the nearest one)?

TUDOR FACT FILE
One of the world's first tennis courts, built by the sporting Henry the Eighth, is still used.

3 Henry was married to his first wife, Catherine of Aragon, for nearly 24 years. He married his second wife, Anne Boleyn, in January 1533. Henry died in January 1547, still married to his sixth wife, Catherine Parr. For how many more years was he married to his first wife than to all the others put together?

CHECK IT YOURSELF ✔

Your answer to 1 ⟶ ☐ ☐ ☐ ☐

Your answer to 2a ⟶ ☐ ☐

Your answer to 2b ⟶ ☐ ☐

Your answer to 3 ⟶ ☐ ☐

Add them   Result ⟶ ☐ ☐ ☐ ☐

Do you get **1899**?
If not, check your answers and try again.

Lovely Grub

The Tudor rich enjoyed eating and showing off their wealth. Here is a menu of a banquet given by King Henry the Eighth.

1st course	2nd course	3rd course
Soup	Soup	Soup
Capon	Capon	Stork
Cygnet	Wren	Pheasant
Venison	Sturgeon	Egret
Pike	Peacock	Chicken
Heron	Pigeon	Gull
Pear pies	Quail	Fried bone-marrow
Custard	Apples	Bream
Fritters	Venison	Oranges
	Tarts	Fritters
	Fritters	

1 How many dishes were there in the first course?

2 How many dishes were there in the second course?

3 How many dishes were there in the third course?

4 How many dishes were there altogether?

5 If each dish in the first course took 10 minutes to serve, eat and clear, how many minutes did the course last?

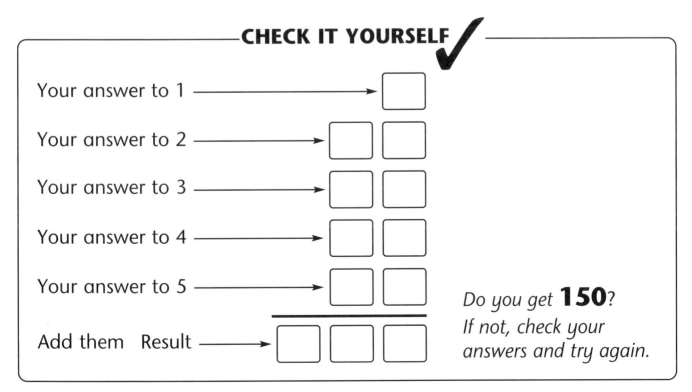

CHECK IT YOURSELF ✔

Your answer to 1 ⟶ ☐

Your answer to 2 ⟶ ☐ ☐

Your answer to 3 ⟶ ☐ ☐

Your answer to 4 ⟶ ☐ ☐

Your answer to 5 ⟶ ☐ ☐

Add them   Result ⟶ ☐ ☐ ☐

Do you get **150**? *If not, check your answers and try again.*

Lovely Grub

The Tudor rich loved eating and showing off their wealth. A banquet combined the two. Here is the menu of a banquet given by King Henry the Eighth.

1st course	2nd course	3rd course
Soup	Soup	Soup
Capon	Capon	Stork
Cygnet	Wren	Pheasant
Venison	Sturgeon	Egret
Pike	Peacock	Chicken
Heron	Pigeon	Gull
Pear pies	Quail	Fried bone-marrow
Custard	Apples	Bream
Fritters	Venison	Oranges
	Tarts	Fritters
	Fritters	

1 If each dish in the first course took 10 minutes to serve, eat and clear, how many hours did the course last?

2 If each dish in the second course took 8 minutes to serve, eat and clear, how many minutes did the course last?

3 If each dish in the third course took 7 minutes to serve, eat and clear, and there were intervals for three songs lasting five minutes each, how many minutes did the course last?

4 If instead the dishes all took 9 minutes each, and there were also a 45-minute interval for dancing and a 50-minute interval for a play, how many minutes did the whole banquet last?

CHECK IT YOURSELF ✔

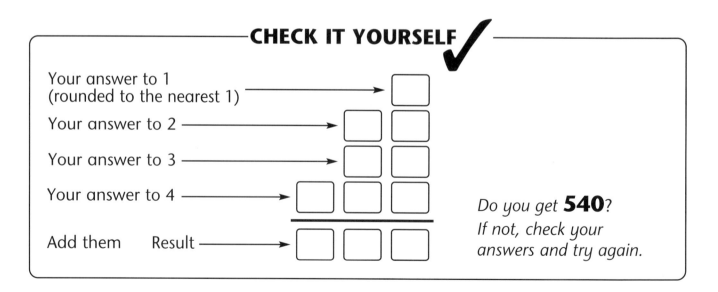

Your answer to 1 (rounded to the nearest 1) →

Your answer to 2 →

Your answer to 3 →

Your answer to 4 →

Add them   Result →

*Do you get **540**? If not, check your answers and try again.*

Revolting Arithmetic: *Tudors*

Lovely Grub

The Tudor rich loved eating and showing off their wealth. A banquet combined the two. Here is the menu of a banquet given by King Henry the Eighth during a conference in France. It had three courses, containing the following dishes:

1st course	2nd course	3rd course
Soup	Soup	Soup
Capon	Capon	Stork
Cygnet	Wren	Pheasant
Venison	Sturgeon	Egret
Pike	Peacock	Chicken
Heron	Pigeon	Gull
Pear pies	Quail	Fried bone-marrow
Custard	Apples	Bream
Fritters	Venison	Oranges
	Tarts	Fritters
	Fritters	

TUDOR FACT FILE
Noblewomen at a banquet measured their importance by the length of the fabric trailing behind their skirt.

1 If each dish in the first course came on platters for 12, and there were 120 guests, how many platters were required for the whole course?

2 If each dish in the second course took 15 minutes to serve, eat and clear, how many minutes did the course last?

3 If each dish in the third course required two cooks to prepare it for half an hour, how many hours of cooks' work was involved?

4 If all the dishes took 12 minutes each, and between courses there were a 45-minute interval for dancing and a 50-minute interval for a play, how long did the banquet last?

CHECK IT YOURSELF ✔

Your answer to 1 ⟶ ☐☐

Your answer to 2 ⟶ ☐☐☐

Your answer to 3 ⟶ ☐☐

Your answer to 4 ⟶ ☐☐☐

Add them   Result ⟶ ☐☐☐

*Do you get **720**?
If not, check your answers and try again.*

The Mary Rose

The *Mary Rose* was Henry the Eighth's favourite battleship. She sank suddenly in 1545, while the King was watching.

STATELLITE
The *Mary Rose* had:
50 small iron guns
15 guns made of bronze

1 How many guns did the *Mary Rose* have altogether?

2 If she had 30 guns on one side, how many cannonballs would be needed to fire them twice?

3 If each gun needed two people to work it, how many people was that?

4 When built, the *Mary Rose* weighed 500 tonnes. When rebuilt, she weighed 700 tonnes. How many tonnes were added to her weight?

5 She was equipped with 200 marines and 30 gunners. How many fighters is that?

CHECK IT YOURSELF ✔

Your answer to 1 ⟶ ☐ ☐

Your answer to 2 ⟶ ☐ ☐

Your answer to 3 ⟶ **1** ☐ ☐

Your answer to 4 ⟶ **2** ☐ ☐

Your answer to 5 ⟶ **2** ☐ ☐

Add them   Result ⟶ **6** ☐ ☐

Do you get **685**?
If not, check your answers and try again.

The Mary Rose

The *Mary Rose* was Henry the Eighth's favourite battleship. She was one of the first ships able to fire a broadside (all the cannon on one side of the ship at the same time). She sank suddenly in 1545, while the King was watching.

STATELLITE
The *Mary Rose* had:
50 small iron guns
15 valuable guns made of bronze

---

1 If five guns faced forwards or backwards, and half the rest faced each side, how many guns did she have in a broadside?

2 If she fired three broadsides, how many cannonballs would be needed?

3 If each gun on the *Mary Rose* needed three people to work it, how many people was that?

4 When built, she weighed 500 tonnes. When rebuilt, she weighed 200 tonnes more. How many tonnes did she weigh when rebuilt?

5 She was equipped with 200 marines and 185 soldiers. How many fighters is that?

CHECK IT YOURSELF ✔

Your answer to 1 ⟶ ☐ ☐

Your answer to 2 ⟶ ☐ ☐

Your answer to 3 ⟶ ☐ ☐ ☐

Your answer to 4 ⟶ ☐ ☐ ☐

Your answer to 5 ⟶ ☐ ☐ ☐

Add them/Result ⟶ ☐ ☐ ☐ ☐

Do you get **1400**?
If not, check your answers and try again.

The Mary Rose

The *Mary Rose* was Henry the Eighth's favourite battleship. She was one of the first ships able to fire a broadside (all the cannon on one side of the ship at the same time). The *Mary Rose* sank suddenly in 1545, while the King was watching. Careless sailors probably left portholes open which let in water.

STATELLITE
The *Mary Rose* had:
50 small iron guns
15 valuable guns made of bronze

1 If three guns were at the bows or stern, and half the rest were facing each side, how many guns did she have in a broadside?

2 If she fired a broadside 15 times, how many cannonballs would be needed?

3 Seven hundred people sailed aboard the *Mary Rose*. If one-quarter of them worked the guns in battle, how many was that?

4 The remains of 500 people were found when her wreck was explored in 1984. How many apparently survived the sinking?

5 She was equipped with 200 marines, 185 soldiers and 30 gunners. How many fighters is that?

CHECK IT YOURSELF ✔

Your answer to 1 ⟶ ☐ ☐

Your answer to 2 ⟶ ☐ ☐ ☐

Your answer to 3 ⟶ ☐ ☐ ☐

Your answer to 4 ⟶ ☐ ☐ ☐

Your answer to 5 ⟶ ☐ ☐ ☐

Add them   Result ⟶ ☐ ☐ ☐ ☐

Do you get **1286**?
If not, check your answers and try again.

All at Sea

A sailor in the Tudor navy was well paid and well fed.

1 If a sailor went on a three-month voyage, how many shillings would he earn?

2 How many pounds of biscuit a day did he get?

3 His ration of biscuit and salt beef came to how many pounds of food a week?

4 How many gallons of beer did he get in two weeks?

STATELLITE
Each month, a sailor earned seven shillings.
Each week, he had
- seven pounds of biscuit
- seven gallons of beer
- eight pounds of salt beef
- some fish, butter and cheese.

TUDOR FACT FILE
Women sailed in warships, too. They cooked, nursed and even disguised themselves as sailor-boys. If a woman had a baby boy on board a warship, he was known as a "son of a gun".

CHECK IT YOURSELF ✔

Your answer to 1 ⟶ ▢ ▢

Your answer to 2 ⟶ ▢

Your answer to 3 ⟶ ▢ ▢

Your answer to 4 ⟶ ▢ ▢

Add them   Result ⟶ ▢ ▢

Do you get **51**?
If not, check your answers and try again.

All at Sea

A sailor in the Tudor navy had a well-paid job and was also well fed. In the 1540s, a sailor could earn in just over two years as much as Sebastian Cabot was paid to explore the Atlantic.

1 If a sailor went on a two-year voyage round the world, how many shillings would he earn?

2 How many pounds of biscuit per week were needed for thirty sailors?

3 How many pints of beer a day did one ration allow (1 gallon = 8 pints)?

4 How many weeks would it take to receive one pound of butter?

STATELLITE
Each month, a sailor earned seven shillings.
Each week, he received
- seven pounds of biscuit
- seven gallons of beer
- eight pounds of salt beef
- a quarter of a pound of butter
- some fish and cheese.

TUDOR FACT FILE
Women sailed in warships, too. They cooked, nursed and even disguised themselves as sailor-boys. If a woman had a baby boy on board a warship, he was known as a "son of a gun".

CHECK IT YOURSELF ✔

Your answer to 1 ⟶ ☐ ☐ ☐

Your answer to 2 ⟶ ☐ ☐ ☐

Your answer to 3 ⟶ ☐

Your answer to 4 ⟶ ☐

Add them   Result ⟶ ☐ ☐ ☐

*Do you get **390**? If not, check your answers and try again.*

All at Sea

Ships were important in Tudor times for trade and defence. A sailor in the Tudor navy had a well-paid job and was also well fed. In the 1540s, a sailor could earn in just over two years as much as Sebastian Cabot was paid to explore the Atlantic.

1 How many months would it take a sailor to earn 168 shillings?

2 How many pounds of biscuit per week were needed for a crew of 175 sailors?

3 How many pints of beer could a sailor drink in a four-week month (1 gallon = 8 pints)?

4 How many pounds of fish would he receive in three months?

STATELLITE

Each month, a sailor earned seven shillings.
Each week, he received
- seven pounds of biscuit
- seven gallons of beer
- eight pounds of salt beef
- three-quarters of a pound of fish
- a quarter of a pound of butter
- three-fifths of a pound of cheese.

TUDOR FACT FILE
Women sailed in warships, too. They cooked, nursed and even disguised themselves as sailor-boys. If a woman had a baby boy on board a warship, he was known as a "son of a gun".

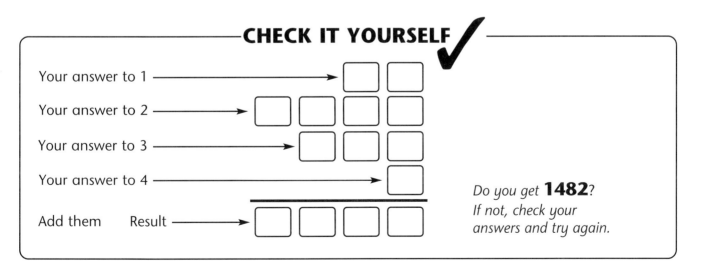

CHECK IT YOURSELF ✔

Your answer to 1 ——————→ ☐ ☐

Your answer to 2 ——→ ☐ ☐ ☐ ☐

Your answer to 3 ——————→ ☐ ☐ ☐

Your answer to 4 ——————————→ ☐

Add them   Result ——————→ ☐ ☐ ☐ ☐

Do you get **1482**?
If not, check your answers and try again.

The Spanish Armada

King Philip the Second of Spain was angry with Queen Elizabeth the First and sent a fleet of ships, called the Armada, to invade England.

1 In what year did the Armada sail? Write it in figures.

2 How many ships sailed in the Spanish Armada? Write it in figures.

3 How many battleships did the Queen have? Write it in figures.

STATELLITE

The Armada sailed in fifteen eighty-eight. Philip's one hundred and thirty-two ships were not a proper battle fleet, and Elizabeth's one hundred and ninety-seven battleships chased them off.
Only 60 ships returned to Spain.
Sir Francis Drake set out to take revenge on Spain with 150 ships. But he lost half his men, 50 ships and £20 000 of the Queen's money.

4 How many ships did Sir Francis Drake return with?

CHECK IT YOURSELF ✔

Your answer to 1 → ☐ ☐ ☐ ☐

Your answer to 2 ——→ ☐ ☐ ☐

Your answer to 3 ——→ ☐ ☐ ☐

Your answer to 4 ——→ ☐ ☐ ☐

Add them Result → **2** ☐ ☐ ☐

Do you get **2017**? *If not, check your answers and try again.*

Revolting Arithmetic: *Tudors*

The Spanish Armada

King Philip the Second of Spain was angry with Queen Elizabeth the First and sent a fleet of ships, called the Armada, to invade England.

STATELLITE
The Armada sailed in 1588. It was not a proper battle fleet and many of the 132 ships were not warships. They carried an army of thirty thousand. Elizabeth's 197 battleships put them to flight. Only 60 ships returned to Spain. Sir Francis Drake set out to take revenge on Spain with 150 ships. But he lost half his men, 50 ships and £20 000 of the Queen's money.

1 How many soldiers sailed with the Armada? Write the number in figures.

2 How many more ships did the Queen have than the King?

3 How many ships were in the battle?

4 How many more ships than the Armada did Drake's revenge fleet have?

5 The Armada fled north. From which direction did the Queen's ships come when they gave chase (N, S, E, W)?

TUDOR FACT FILE
In 1587, Sir Francis Drake had sailed into Cadiz harbour, where the Spanish fleet was being assembled. He sank many ships and burned thousands of tonnes of supplies. "I have singed the King of Spain's beard," he said.

CHECK IT YOURSELF ✔

Your answer to 1 ⟶ ☐ ☐ ☐ ☐ ☐

Your answer to 2 ⟶ ☐ ☐

Your answer to 3 ⟶ ☐ ☐ ☐

Your answer to 4 ⟶ ☐ ☐

Your answer to 5 ⟶ ☐
(key N=1, S=2, E=3, W=4)

Add them   Result ⟶ **3** **0** ☐ ☐ ☐

Do you get **30 414**? *If not, check your answers and try again.*

The Spanish Armada

3

King Philip the Second of Spain was angry with Queen Elizabeth the First and sent a fleet of ships, called the Armada, to invade England.

STATELLITE

The Armada sailed in 1588. It was not a proper battle fleet. Sailing among the warships were hulks, armed cargo ships, grain ships and galleys powered by oars. The 132 ships carried an army of 30 000. Elizabeth's 197 nimble battleships put them to flight. Only 60 ships returned to Spain. But Sir Francis Drake, the battle hero, set out with 150 ships to take revenge on Spain. He lost half his 15 000 men, as well as 50 ships and £20 000 of the Queen's money.

---

1 If the Queen lost one ship in five, how many is that, in round numbers?

2 If an average of just nine fighters in each of the Queen's ships were injured in battle, how many does that make?

3 If all the ships engaged in battle fired just eight shots each, how many cannonballs would that take?

4 If one in six of the ships lost by the Spanish Armada made it to a foreign harbour, how many arrived?

TUDOR FACT FILE

In 1587, Sir Francis Drake had sailed into Cadiz harbour, where the Spanish fleet was being assembled. In a two-day battle, he sank scores of ships and burned thousands of tonnes of supplies. "I have singed the King of Spain's beard," he famously remarked.

CHECK IT YOURSELF ✔

Your answer to 1 ⟶ ☐ ☐

Your answer to 2 ⟶ ☐ ☐ ☐

Your answer to 3 ⟶ ☐ ☐ ☐ ☐

Your answer to 4 ⟶ ☐ ☐

Add them   Result ⟶ ☐ ☐ ☐ ☐

Do you get **4456**?
If not, check your answers and try again.

Tudor Theatre

In Tudor times, the theatre was very popular. Many of the best plays were signed by William Shakespeare. Here is a list of his comedies.

The Two Gentlemen of Verona	Twelfth Night
The Taming of the Shrew	Troilus and Cressida
The Comedy of Errors	Measure for Measure
Love's Labour's Lost	All's Well That Ends Well
A Midsummer Night's Dream	Pericles, Prince of Tyre
The Merchant of Venice	The Winter's Tale
The Merry Wives of Windsor	Cymbeline
Much Ado About Nothing	The Tempest
As You Like It	

1 How many comedies are listed?

2 The last four plays were probably written after Queen Elizabeth died. How many were written during her reign?

3 If a comedy lasted 100 minutes and there were two intervals of 15 minutes, how many minutes did a whole show last?

4 Shakespeare signed 38 plays altogether. How many others is that, besides these comedies?

CHECK IT YOURSELF ✔

Your answer to 1 ⟶ ☐ ☐

Your answer to 2 ⟶ ☐ ☐

Your answer to 3 ⟶ ☐ ☐ ☐

Your answer to 4 ⟶ ☐ ☐

Add them   Result ⟶ ☐ ☐ ☐

Do you get **181**?
If not, check your answers and try again.

Tudor Theatre

In Tudor times, the theatre was very popular. Women's roles were played by boys. Many of the best plays were signed by William Shakespeare. Here is a list of his comedies and tragedies.

Comedies	
The Two Gentlemen of Verona	As You Like It
The Taming of the Shrew	Twelfth Night
The Comedy of Errors	Troilus and Cressida
Love's Labour's Lost	Measure for Measure
A Midsummer Night's Dream	All's Well That Ends Well
The Merchant of Venice	Pericles, Prince of Tyre
The Merry Wives of Windsor	The Winter's Tale
Much Ado About Nothing	Cymbeline
	The Tempest

Tragedies		
Titus Andronicus	Hamlet	Macbeth
Romeo and Juliet	Othello	Antony and Cleopatra
Julius Caesar	Timon of Athens	Coriolanus
	King Lear	

1 How many more comedies than tragedies were signed by William Shakespeare?

2 Four of these plays were probably written after Queen Elizabeth died. How many were written during her reign?

3 If a comedy or tragedy lasted two hours, how many hours of entertainment does this list represent?

4 Shakespeare signed 38 plays altogether. How many others is that, besides these comedies and tragedies?

CHECK IT YOURSELF ✔

Your answer to 1 ⟶ ☐

Your answer to 2 ⟶ ☐ ☐

Your answer to 3 ⟶ ☐ ☐

Your answer to 4 ⟶ ☐ ☐

Add them   Result ⟶ ☐ ☐

*Do you get **95**? If not, check your answers and try again.*

Tudor Theatre

During Elizabeth's reign, the theatre was very popular. Women's roles were played by boys. Many of the best plays were signed by William Shakespeare. Here is a list of his comedies and tragedies.

Comedies
The Two Gentlemen of Verona	As You Like It
The Taming of the Shrew	Twelfth Night
The Comedy of Errors	Troilus and Cressida
Love's Labour's Lost	Measure for Measure
A Midsummer Night's Dream	All's Well That Ends Well
The Merchant of Venice	Pericles, Prince of Tyre
The Merry Wives of Windsor	The Winter's Tale
Much Ado About Nothing	Cymbeline
	The Tempest

Tragedies
Titus Andronicus	Hamlet	Macbeth
Romeo and Juliet	Othello	Antony and Cleopatra
Julius Caesar	Timon of Athens	Coriolanus
	King Lear	

1 How many comedies and tragedies were signed by William Shakespeare?

2 The plays lasted about 1.5 hours each. How many hours of **tragedy** are represented in this list?

3 If a comedy or tragedy had two 15-minute intervals added, how many hours did it last?

4 Shakespeare signed 38 plays altogether. How many hours of complete performances (plays plus intervals) is that?

CHECK IT YOURSELF ✓

Your answer to 1 ⟶ ☐ ☐

Your answer to 2 ⟶ ☐ ☐

Your answer to 3 ⟶ ☐

Your answer to 4 ⟶ ☐ ☐

Add them   Result ⟶ ☐ ☐ ☐

*Do you get **120**? If not, check your answers and try again.*

Answers

Bosworth Field

Level 1
1. 2000
2. 750 + 95 = 845
3. 10 ÷ 5 = 2
4. $1 - \frac{1}{2} = \frac{1}{2}$

Level 2
1. 12 090
2. 758 + 396 = 1154
3. 900 − 250 = 650
4. 1 − 0.5 = 0.5

Level 3
1. 12 090 − 2028 = 10 062
2. 1400 + 1650 = 3050
3. 1000 − 20% = 1000 − [$\frac{1}{5}$ x 1000 = 200] = 1000 − 200 = 800
4. 12 000 x 50% = 12 000 x $\frac{1}{2}$ = 6000

Lavish Living

Level 1
1. 12 x 2 = 24
2. 8 x 2 = 16
3. 1 + 10 = 11 x 2 = 22
4. 1 + 1 = 2 x 7 = 14

Level 2
1. 12 x 2 = 24 x 7 = 168
2. 8 x 2 = 16 x 7 = 112
3. 1 + 10 = 11 x 2 = 22 x 7 = 154
4. 6 x 12 = 72 ÷ 11 = 6.5 = 7
5. 15 x 2 = 30 x 7 = 210

Level 3
1. 12 x 2 = 24 x 7 = 168 ÷ 11 = 15.27 = 15
2. 8 x 2 = 16 x 7 = 112 ÷ 11 = 10.18 = 10
3. $16 - 7\frac{1}{2} = 8\frac{1}{2} \times 7 = 59\frac{1}{2}$
4. 6 x 50 = 300 ÷ 11 = 27.27 = 27
5. 15 x 2 = 30 x 14 = 420

Monks and Money

Level 1
1. 1517
2. 40 + 40 + 40 = 120
3. 765 + 98 = 863
4. 13

Level 2
1. 45 x 0.5 = 45 ÷ 2 = 22.5
2. 4 + 2 + 3 = 9 x 45 = 405
3. 765 + 398 = 1163
4. 500 + 556 = 1056

Level 3
1. 37 x 50% = 37 ÷ 2 = 18.50
2. 4 + 2 + 7 = 13 x 37 = 481
3. 1765 + 1398 = 3163
4. 500 − 37 = 463

Answers

Greedy Henry

Level 1
1. $1 - \frac{1}{4} = \frac{3}{4}$
2. 1012
3. 30 − 10 = 20
4. 985 + 95 = 1080

Level 2
1. 1 − 0.3 = 0.7
2. 807 + 205 = 1012
3. 375 + 242 + 400 + 600 = 1617
4. 986 + 765 = 1751

Level 3
1. 100 − 25 = 75
2. 1012 − 807 = 205
3. 1375 + 242 + 1400 + 2600 = 5617
4. 1387 + 1899 = 3286

Pilgrimage of Grace

Level 1
1. 74 + 83 = 157
2. 74 + 83 + 59 + 34 = 250
3. 976
4. 250 − 35 = 215

Level 2
1. 108 + 129 = 237
2. 237 + 96 + 42 = 375
3. 40 000
4. 96 − [96 ÷ 4 = 24] = 96 − 24 = 72

Level 3
1. 1108 + 1129 = 2237
2. 2237 + 796 + 242 = 3275
3. 40 000 − 3275 = 36 725
4. 796 − [796 × $\frac{1}{4}$ = 796 ÷ 4 = 199]
   = 796 − 199 = 597

Thomas Cromwell

Level 1
1. 920
2. 59 + 31 + 28 = 118
3. 1535 + 4 = 1539
4. 6

Level 2
1. 920 + 119 = 1039
2. 28 ÷ 4 = 7
3. 1539 − 1535 = 4
4. 258 + 983 = 1241

Level 3
1. 920 ÷ 4 = 230
2. 59 + 31 + 28 = 118 ÷ 4
   = 29 remainder 2
3. 1098 + 3499 = 4597
4. 8000 ÷ 25 = 320

Answers

Tudor Punishments

Level 1
1 2 + 3 + 1 + 2 = 8
2 30 + 50 = 80
3 5 + 7 + 14 + 25 = 51
4 24 + 24 + 24 = 72

Level 2
1 2 + 3 + 1 + 2 = 8 x 24 = 192
2 130 + 150 = 280
3a 5 + 7 + 14 + 25 = 51 x 5 = 255
3b 24 + 24 + 24 = 72 x 5 = 360
3c 12 x 5 = 60 x 4 = 240

Level 3
1 2 + 3 + 1 + 2 = 8 x 24 = 192 x 5 = 960
2 130 + 150 = 280 x 5 = 1400
3 5 + 7 + 14 + 25 = 51 x 5 = 255 x 4 = 1020
4 24 + 24 + 24 = 72 x 5 = 360 x 4 = 1440
5 12 x 5 = 60 x 4 = 240 x 6 = 1440

Henry the Eighth

Level 1
1 160
2 205
3 24 – 10 = 14

Level 2
1 30 x 5 = 150
2 51 x 4 = 204
3 1547 – 1533 = 14 + 24 = 38

Level 3
1 5 x 365 = 1825
2a 204 ÷ 4 = 51
2b 51 ÷ 4 = 12.75 = 13
3 1547 – 1533 = 14; 24 – 14 = 10

Lovely Grub

Level 1
1 9
2 11
3 10
4 9 + 11 + 10 = 30
5 9 x 10 = 90

Level 2
1 9 x 10 = 90 ÷ 60 = $1\frac{1}{2}$ [= 2]
2 11 x 8 = 88
3 10 x 7 = 70 + 5 + 5 + 5 = 85
4 9 + 11 + 10 = 30 x 9
= 270 + 45 + 50 = 365

Level 3
1 9 x [120 ÷ 12 = 10] = 9 x 10 = 90
2 11 x 15 = 165
3 2 x $\frac{1}{2}$ = 1 x 10 = 10
4 9 + 11 + 10 = 30 x 12
= 360 + 45 + 50 = 455

Answers

The *Mary Rose*

Level 1
1. 50 + 15 = 65
2. 30 + 30 = 60
3. 65 + 65 = 130
4. 700 − 500 = 200
5. 200 + 30 = 230

Level 2
1. 50 + 15 = 65 − 5 = 60 ÷ 2 = 30
2. 30 x 3 = 90
3. 65 x 3 = 195
4. 500 + 200 = 700
5. 200 + 185 = 385

Level 3
1. 50 + 15 = 65 − 3 = 62 ÷ 2 = 31
2. 31 x 15 = 465
3. 700 ÷ 4 = 175
4. 700 − 500 = 200
5. 200 + 185 + 30 = 415

All at Sea

Level 1
1. 7 x 3 = 21
2. 7 ÷ 7 = 1
3. 7 + 8 = 15
4. 7 x 2 = 14

Level 2
1. 7 x 24 = 168
2. 7 x 30 = 210
3. 7 ÷ 7 = 1 x 8 = 8
4. 4

Level 3
1. 168 ÷ 7 = 24
2. 7 x 175 = 1225
3. 7 x 8 = 56 x 4 = 224
4. 3 x 4 = 12 x $\frac{3}{4}$ = 12 ÷ 4 = 3 x 3 = 9

The Spanish Armada

Level 1
1. 1588
2. 132
3. 197
4. 150 − 50 = 100

Level 2
1. 30 000
2. 197 − 132 = 65
3. 197 + 132 = 329
4. 150 − 132 = 18
5. S = 2

Level 3
1. 197 ÷ 5 = 39.4 = 39
2. 197 x 9 = 1773
3. 197 + 132 = 329 x 8 = 2632
4. 132 − 60 = 72 ÷ 6 = 12

Answers

Tudor Theatre

Level 1
1. 17
2. 17 − 4 = 13
3. 100 + [15 + 15 = 30]
   = 100 + 30 = 130
4. 38 − 17 = 21

Level 2
1. 17 − 10 = 7
2. [17 + 10] − 4 = 27 − 4 = 23
3. 27 x 2 = 54
4. 38 − 27 = 11

Level 3
1. 17 + 10 = 27
2. 1.5 x 10 = 15
3. [15 + 15] + 90 = 30 + 90
   = 120 ÷ 60 = 2
4. 38 x 2 = 76